I0173170

Metamorphosis

Poems about betrayal, grief, and healing.

Anna Charlotte Sommer

BookLeaf
Publishing

India | USA | UK

Made with ❤ on the BookLeaf Publishing Platform
www.bookleafpub.in
www.bookleafpub.com

Dedication

This book is dedicated to anyone who has been broken open by betrayal and wondered if they would ever feel whole again. May these words offer you company in the dark, and light enough to find your way to the truth of your own heart, to the tenderness that still lives beneath the ache, to the version of you that feels like home.

Preface

These poems began as fragments scribbled in the quiet hours, when language was the only thing that could hold me and tears were my steady companion. In time, writing became less about the one who caused the wound and more about learning to live beyond it — allowing grief to teach me alchemy, so I could burn away old beliefs about love, loss, and who I thought I was.

The body remembers what the mind cannot name. Each poem is a pulse, a tremor, a breath — the body's way of telling the truth. Through writing, I learned to listen to those truths, to give shape to the unspeakable, to find tenderness in the scars.

Betrayal rearranges the map of the heart. It asks us to walk barefoot through the ruins and discover what still lives there. These poems were born from that walk — from the ache and the quiet, from the slow reweaving of trust in myself, in love, and in life itself.

Acknowledgements

To the ones who witnessed my breaking and believed in my becoming, thank you for your light in the dark. To the body, the breath, and the earth beneath me — thank you for carrying me home. And to the quiet hours, the patient page, and the pulse of life that kept whispering "keep going" — I am endlessly grateful.

1. Polaroid in Reverse

With other things,
the event becomes an anchor point—

a way to look back and say
oh, that's what happened,
and this is how my life pivoted into the now.

It doesn't make the event
any more digestible,
but it offers something to orient around—
a sense of cause and effect,
before and after,

a distinguishable mark
on the timeline of life,
where the timeline itself remains intact
despite the change in direction.

But this—
this betrayal—

there is nothing solid about this.
The timeline I thought was there
never actually existed,

and I am left sifting
through tiny drops of truth,
some from you,
some I found on my own,
and some that remain invisible,

because reality is almost impossible
to reconstruct in hindsight
when it was kept hidden from you.

I keep trying to collect those drops,
find more truth,
and contain them
in some way that makes sense—

but I find the container of my mind
inadequate to hold them,
or form anything solid.

It's all just a hologram
of what I thought my life was,
all those days I thought
I was building it with him.

And every time I reach back
and try to touch it,

my hand slips through—

I am left holding elusiveness,
feeling its molecules
run through my fingers,
with nothing to tether themselves to.

Stolen memories
are more slippery than water.
There is no amount of chasing
that will save them,
no enclosure
that can hold them safely.

And so we float,
haphazardly for a while—
my memories and I—
reaching for each other
in slow motion,

as I watch each drop
of what I thought my life was
dissipate steadily,
like Polaroid pictures in reverse.

2. Other Women

I heard the faint whisper of other women
the last time I laid on his chest.

His heartbeat tried to muffle their voices,
but a heart's rhythm made from lies
can only hide so much.

One woman was laughing.

One was moaning from his touch.

One was telling him
why she was better than me.

One tried hiding
behind her own silence.

Another let excuses and justification
speak for her.

One was drunk
and too embarrassed to say anything.

And one just rambled on

about everything that was wrong with me
despite not knowing me at all.

Sometimes I wonder if they are still there,
trying to speak,
keeping time by his heartbeat,
trapped under the weight of their own decisions.

3. What Could Have Been

sometimes

late at night,

when the portal to what could have been cracks open,
I step inside and look for you.

I take hold of that silvery, hope-filled thread
and swing between moments that never became
and memories that will never be.

like that one morning
when you pulled me off the couch,
and we slow danced in the living room
to a song that could only be heard between us—
and you looked so deeply into my eyes
that I could see myself
the way you saw me,
and I knew I would always be safe with you.

or the year we bought an old camper
and drove to every state (almost) with our kids,
visiting national parks,
meeting bugs and rocks and rivers

that became our friends,
and collecting refrigerator magnets
from every place we went
so we could point to them and say—
remember when we went there...

or all the days we sat together on the front porch,
gray hairs and laugh lines measuring time passed,
our hands still finding ways
to weave themselves together,
as a way to say—
thank you for loving me all these years.

sometimes I try to grab onto
a memory that never was,
but they are not solid enough to grasp,
and their inability to be true
sends me back into reality
with a flavor of grief
that I can never rinse away.

4. Mistaken

Your love came wrapped in chaos and deception.
It felt familiar in both its offering
and in my ability to stay small enough to take it in.

That's what I thought I deserved,

wounded love
trying to soothe
wounded ideas of being loved.

Maybe that's where I was mistaken.

Maybe deserving is nothing more than
what we believe we are worthy of
and what we are willing to accept.

5. Sacred Rage

I heard a knock at the door.

Not gentle.
Not malicious.

Strong.
Determined.

Like a gust of wind
that brings with it
a change in the weather.

I opened the door—
both knowing
and not knowing what to expect.

On the other side was Rage,
cloaked in red,
taller than me,
taller than I remember.

I invited her in
and we sat down for tea.

She did not sit quietly
and discuss things
in a civilized manner.

Nor did she lash out
in a childish attempt at revenge.

Her eyes were dark
but full of color,
and open very, very wide.

They held a clarity
that could not be argued with.

Within them,
I saw where I was giving my power away—
unconsciously drawing a line in the sand
with a trembling hand,
and then erasing it with the other,

because I did not believe
I deserved to hold the line.

I did not believe
I deserved to be respected
or loved
or tended to

in a way that was truly safe.

And when Rage saw this happening,
she began to rise like a flame—
heated with wisdom,
and sharp like an arrow,
aimed directly at my pain.

But I held up my shaking hand
in protest.

Hushhh, I said.
Be quiet.
Don't make such a fuss.

And I allowed him to see
that there was no longer
a line in the sand—
that it was okay
to love me
with hurtful words
and dishonest actions.

I let him cut me down
until there was nothing left of me
that I could recognize—

just broken and muddled pieces,
with no understanding
of how to begin again.

Rage came over
and poured me another cup of tea.

She spoke with authority,
her tone holding my attention
like a mother holding a wounded child—
both arms
a steady definition
of love and protection.

And then I understood
that it was her all along—
that she was the line in the sand.

And I understood
what it meant
to trust her
and allow her
to work through me.

But because I betrayed her
and deemed her irrelevant,
she could not stand up for me,

or protect me,
or offer me her clarity
to help me see
all the ways I was being betrayed by him.

And so I looked her in the eyes
and deemed her Sacred—
and we became friends.

6. Two Roads

I was a portal
through which you could become
a better version of yourself.

And you were mine.

I thought our relationship
was divinely orchestrated.
I thought that meant
we were supposed to rise—together—
lifting each other as we climbed.

We were both the path
and the purpose for each other.

Only you had other plans—
or maybe you were just scared—
so you decided to walk on two roads:
one meant to elevate,
and one meant to go nowhere.

Although I couldn't see
that you had one foot
firmly planted on each road,

I could feel the weight of it.

And when I asked,
you thought it best to keep things hidden,
to bargain with the truth.

Every step I thought
we were taking together
was weighed down
with your foot on the other road—
your decision to go nowhere.

I could feel the heaviness of your secrets,
despite not knowing
the burden of your betrayal for years.

And eventually,
when it all came to light,
I saw that I could be my own portal.

I gave myself
a quiet permission
to walk the road without you,
finding strength in my bones—
built from carrying
the potential of us.

It wasn't until I took
my first step forward
that I realized:

the portal wasn't opened
in us coming together—
it was opened
in letting each other go.

7. Scars

Every time I try to reach for you,

my hands brush
over the scars you left behind—

the ones that have healed,

and the ones
that still break open and bleed,
no matter
how much time has passed.

8. What I Thought Love Was

You broke my heart,
again and again.

And I let you break it,
over and over.

Because that's what I thought love was.

Staying small,

and desperately reaching for hope
while reality was spitting in my face.

9. Unseen

very slowly and quietly

over many, many days

I began dying

until I was completely gone.
and because it wasn't loud or sudden—

because it looked like I was still breathing,
because I kept a smile on my face
and said I was fine,
because I kept up
with the day-to-day of things—

no one noticed
I wasn't alive anymore.

10. Knives and Spoons

You didn't just have an affair.

Or several.

You let other women
into the home
I was trying to build with you.

You opened the door
with secrets and lies,
and invited them inside.

They came with spoons
that fed your hungry ego,
and you offered them knives
to slit me open.

I bled for years
not knowing the origin of my wounds,
finding drops of blood
on the carpet.

Each time I pointed to a stain
and pleaded for you

to tell me where it came from,

you lied,
you said you didn't know,
you twisted the truth,

pointing back at me
and telling me I was crazy,
that I was the problem.

And I swallowed every word.

11. Hidden

Sometimes I wonder
if I ever truly loved you
the way you needed to be loved.

I only ever saw half of you.

The rest was hidden,
tucked away
under the floorboards
in a secret room.

You were good at hiding.

And no matter
how intensely I tried to seek,
my calls for *Marco*
never heard the echo of *Polo.*

My sometimes gentle
and sometimes fierce tugging
at the knot in your heart
made you pull away even more.

I think that is what I grieve the most—

the chance I never had
to hold all of you in my being.

To truly see you.
To fully know you.
To honestly love you.

12. The Quiet Pause

In the quiet pause

between inhale and exhale—

where I wanted
to hold my breath
a little longer,

but didn't,

I found you for a moment,
remembering how much I miss you.

Not loudly.

Softly.

With reverence.

Where no one noticed but me.

13. I Don't Hate You

I don't hate you.

I hate what you did,
and I hate that you did it
repeatedly for years.

I hate that your behavior
caused me to question
my value as a human being.

I hate that you looked me in the eyes
and lied—
then kept lying
even when I started seeing the truth.

I hate that you were supposed to be my shield,
and you ended up being
the sword I didn't see coming.

I hate that you made me believe
in a future that was never going to exist,
and you became a part of my past
that I could only clearly see
in hindsight.

I hate how careless you were with my heart—
that the sound of it breaking
over and over
wasn't enough
to make you stop.

I hate that you couldn't offer respect
when I tried to love you,
and that you couldn't offer dignity
when I tried to recover from you.

I hate that you were at war with yourself,
and that you made me the enemy
in a battle
I didn't know I was fighting.

I don't hate you.
I never could.

I hate what you did,
and I hate that you didn't choose me,
and I hate that the only way
to heal from this
is to choose myself.

14. Forgiveness

To the man I loved
and all the women he cheated on me with:

I hope,
with everything in my being,

that one day
your life will have more fulfilled dreams
than you can imagine right now—

that you are thriving
in ways you didn't think were possible,

that you are so happy
the idea of treating another human
in the selfish, hurtful, and damaging ways
that you did

will never again
be a thought in your mind.

15. Letting Go

Perhaps we let go slowly,

carefully,

with reverence
for the departure.

Perhaps we unravel things
gently,

together,

in a way
that only makes sense to us.

Perhaps instead of feeding resentment,
we send an invitation
for healing to visit.

And when she stops by,

perhaps we invite her in,

and let her show us

how we've hurt each other,
where our wounds
are still open and raw.

Perhaps we offer each other salve
in the form of forgiveness—

and let healing finish
what love began.

16. Polishing Grief

If grief were a stone,
I would carry it in my pocket—

and hope that I could live a life
with only a few tiny pebbles
held tightly there.

But most lives, if not all,
will find pockets lined with many stones,
all holding the unique shape of what was lost,
and the weight of healing
that needs to be cultivated.

If grief were a stone,
I would carry it in my pocket,

bracing for impact
every time a wave came crashing over me—
except, of course,
for those waves I don't see coming,

the ones that pull me down deep,
where oxygen is sparse,
and survival seems unlikely.

If grief were a stone,
I would carry it in my pocket,

along with a few grains of hope
that, somehow, little by little,
I could polish down the sharp edges,

and learn how to hold it with grace,
so that both the stone and I
could soften
in the way we respond to each other.

If grief were a stone,
I would carry it in my pocket,

and hope that near the end of my time here,
I could reach my hand in
and find your stone—

smoothed over from years of tending to it,
washed clean from tears,
and much, much lighter
for having loved
and carried it so thoughtfully.

17. Healing

Healing asks everything of you.

To show up.

To answer her call
when you're bruised
and broken
and barely breathing.

To arrive exactly where you are
and tell her you are ready.

Then show up again.
And again.
And again.

Healing asks you to surrender.

To soften.
To allow.
To crack open
in ways that seem unrecoverable at times.

And to trust

that she has a map
leading you back to yourself.

Healing asks you to walk barefoot
beyond anything familiar or comfortable,

and pitch a tent
in the wilderness of the unknown.

Then do it again
as soon as you are resting easy there.

She asks you to liberate
the parts of yourself you kept hidden
in order to feel loved.

To feel everything.
I mean everything.

To feel it
in the darkest parts of your bones,
and in every chamber of your heart.

Healing asks you to rethink every thought
and revisit every belief.

To sift through all the memories and moments

you thought were lost
in the web of your mind—

the ones that beg to be seen
and untangled from your history,
so they can help transform your future.

Healing asks you to be brave.

To look every monster in the eyes.

To see that they are the parts of you
that feel scared
or unsafe
or full of shame.

To understand
that their growls and roars
are really cries
to be held and seen.

Healing asks you to move.

To dance.
To shake yourself alive again.

She asks you to be still.

To go inward.
To notice with quiet intention.

Healing asks you to be curious.

To be open.
To question the very ground
you've been standing on.

To believe that something else is possible—
that more than pain exists.

To release the idea
that all this is happening *to* you
instead of *through* you.

Healing asks you to ground yourself in truth.

To allow the most authentic parts of you
a seat at the table.

To hold up a microphone
and let the realness of your being
sing you awake.

Healing asks you to create.

To paint or write or garden—
to do anything
that brings you little bits of joy.

She asks you to hold her hand
and pull her through your very being,
so that she can be reborn through you,
infused in all your passions and dreams.

Healing asks you to carry your pain like a child,
and tend to its every need.

And then she asks you
to allow your life to grow around your pain—

to alchemize it
into the very medicine you needed,
and the very medicine
you are meant to share with the world.

Healing asks you to give a voice
to everything you once silenced.

To be honest.
To be vulnerable.

To let the raw truth of you

pour out in every word—

to be so bold with your voice
that every version of you that came before,
and every version you are becoming,
can hear you.

And nothing is lost in translation.

Healing asks you to read your story out loud.

Even if no one is listening.
Especially if no one is listening.

She asks you to read your own memoir
as if it were unknown to you—

to understand it
from a different perspective,
to see it with fresh eyes.

And then write it again
from where you are now,

as if it were
the very thing
that will liberate you completely.

18. Matamorphosis

The reason you smile
every time you see a butterfly

is because somewhere in your being
you recognize the joy
that comes from understanding

that metamorphosis
is not the same
as being destroyed.

19. The Fragrance of Memory

We are not meant
to hold onto the people
we love the most.

They are a passing force
in our world,

as we are in theirs.

And when they leave,

if we are lucky,

their essence remains
like a fragrance.

The wholeness of their existence
becomes a drop of perfume

left on our skin,
lingering boldly
in every inhale.

20. Threshold

I stood at the edge of change,

not knowing how I got there,
but knowing it was where I needed to be—

feet planted in the earth,
dirt mushed between my toes,
looking out into the void
and shivering with indecision.

Everything in front of me was nameless,
without form
or context of any kind,
and smelled vaguely
of a memory
of having been here before.

Everything behind me
was woven with familiarity,
offering threads to grasp
that would lead me back
to an old version of myself—

one who was scared,

or lonely,
or trying to keep me away from the edge.

Thank you, I whispered,
to all the versions of me
I had been before.

And I jumped into the void,
surrendering to my own undoing—

smiling,
not knowing how to fly,
but knowing
my own center of gravity
would not betray me.

21. Unleashed

something in me needed to scream

to let rage have a voice,

so I went into the woods
and unleashed myself.

I thought I would be alone in this,

but the trees circled around me
and carried my cries to the sky,

and my ancestors stood among the ferns,
singing me on in celebration—

because I became the one
who refused to believe
that silence and safety
are synonymous.

22. Let Me Be

Let me be earth.

Let me be so rooted
that I have no choice
but to rise.

Let me be air.

Let me breathe in
all I have forsaken,
so that every exhale
is a prayer of gratitude.

Let me be fire.

Let me burn away
all the beliefs
that have overgrown my path.

Let me be water.

Let me flow with ease
into my own becoming.

Let me be aether.

Let me rest
in the space between all things,
in the breath between words
where silence becomes song
and every ending hums
with beginning.

www.ingramcontent.com/pod-product-compliance
Lightning Source LLC
Chambersburg PA
CBHW070500050426
42449CB00012B/3061